Author:

Rupert Matthews was born in Surrey, England, in 1961. He was educated at his local grammar school and has made a lifelong study of history. He has written more than 150 books since becoming a full-time writer.

Artist:

Mark Bergin was born in Hastings, England, in 1961. He studied at Eastbourne College of Art and specializes in historical reconstructions, aviation, and maritime subjects. He lives in Bexhill-on-Sea with his wife and children.

Series creator:

David Salariya was born in Dundee, Scotland. He has illustrated a wide range of books and has created and designed many new series for publishers in the UK and overseas. In 1989, he established The Salariya Book Company. He lives in Brighton, England, with his wife, illustrator Shirley Willis, and their son, Jonathan.

Editor: **Tanya Kant**

Editorial assistant: **Mark Williams**

PAPER FROM
SUSTAINABLE
FORESTS

Published in Great Britain in 2010 by
The Salariya Book Company Ltd
25 Marlborough Place, Brighton BN1 1UB

ISBN-13: 978-0-531-20470-2 (lib. bdg.)   978-0-531-22825-8 (pbk.)
ISBN-10: 0-531-20470-7 (lib. bdg.)   0-531-22825-8 (pbk.)

All rights reserved.
Published in 2010 in the United States
by Franklin Watts
An imprint of Scholastic Inc.
557 Broadway, New York, NY 10012
Published simultaneously in Canada.

A CIP catalog record for this book is available
from the Library of Congress.

Printed and bound in Heshan, China.
Printed on paper from sustainable sources.
1 2 3 4 5 6 7 8 9 10 R 18 17 16 15 14 13 12 11 10 09

You Wouldn't Want to Be a Chicago Gangster!

Written by
Rupert Matthews

Illustrated by
Mark Bergin

Created and designed by
David Salariya

Some Dangerous Characters You'd Better Avoid

Franklin Watts®
An Imprint of Scholastic Inc.
NEW YORK • TORONTO • LONDON • AUCKLAND • SYDNEY
MEXICO CITY • NEW DELHI • HONG KONG
DANBURY, CONNECTICUT

Contents

Introduction 5

Looking for Work 6

Into the Gang 8

Numbers Racket 10

The Gambling Den 12

Spying in the Speakeasy 14

Due North 16

The Wheelman 18

Running the Protection Racket 20

Packing Heat 22

Money Laundering 24

The Boss 26

Final Reckoning 28

Glossary 30

Index 32

Introduction

The year is 1925, and you and your brother, Tony, are living in Chicago, Illinois—a city that's notorious for its ruthless gangsters.

In fact, throughout the United States, organized crime is on the rise. In 1920, the government made it illegal to own or sell alcoholic drinks, a law referred to as "Prohibition."

After the law was passed, gangs of criminals realized they could make big money by manufacturing, importing, and selling alcohol throughout the country. And lots of these gangsters are right here in Chicago.

Police officers stage raids to find and destroy alcohol.

This is you.   *This is your brother, Tony.*

Looking for Work

You and Tony have your own problems. He's just lost his job. And you just graduated, so you're looking to land a job as well.

Both of you have pounded the pavement every day, but so far, neither of you has had any luck. You guys are quickly running out of money—and you're getting desperate. You're both willing to try ANYTHING.

Here are some of the jobs that you and Tony tried to get:

THE MOVIE STUDIOS in Hollywood, California, provide work for lots of people. But first you have to get there. Can't afford the train fare? Tough! The conductor won't let you travel.

No money, no travel!

What's that for?

YOU'VE HEARD there's work on the farms in the countryside outside Chicago. But you grew up in the city—you don't have a clue about farming!

It's not what you know, it's who you know.

FACTORIES often need workers. But they mostly hire experienced laborers or people who are recommended by other employees. If you don't know anyone at the factory, forget it!

YOU COULD WORK in a store, but most are family businesses. You'll get a job only if a relative owns the place. Born into the wrong family? Then you're out of luck.

Into the Gang

Tony decides that you should both join the police force. The Chicago police need people who are tough, honest, and know the area. Even better, you don't need lots of experience—they'll train you once you've got the job. They will even issue you a sharp new uniform, so you won't need to buy new clothes.

Tony gets a job patrolling the streets of Chicago, and you volunteer to work undercover. You're going to pretend to be a Chicago gangster! But it's dangerous work. If the gangsters learn that you're working for the police, you'll be in big trouble.

YOU START your undercover career as a street sweeper. That way, you can watch the gangsters in action, but no one will pay attention to you.

Don't ask any questions, kid.

THANKS TO HIS fancy clothes and car, the local gangster boss should be easy to spot. Treat him with respect—hold his car door open for him.

THE GANGSTER decides that he likes you, so he asks you to do him a favor—deliver a package to a certain address. But he doesn't pay you—at least, not yet.

YOU KEEP your brother, Tony, informed about what the gangsters are doing. You show him the package that you have to deliver so he can add it to his report.

TONY PATROLS the streets that you clean, so you often bump into each other. Pretend you don't know him, and try to look as if you have something to hide. Gangsters aren't supposed to be on good terms with police officers.

Numbers Racket

The gangsters give you your first job—you'll be running an illegal gambling operation on the streets. This "numbers racket" involves only small amounts of money, so it's a good way for the gang to find out whether you can be trusted—without risking too much cash. Most of the bets you take are on horse races. You need to be able to add numbers quickly so that you can keep track of the betting odds, people's bets, and how much they have won—or lost.

GAMBLING is illegal, and only Tony knows you are undercover. Any other police officer will try to arrest you.

ALL THE BETS are made in cash. Your job is to make a profit, so don't offer generous odds—the local boss doesn't want to pay out too much money if a gambler wins a bet. You hand over the profits to the gang immediately. If you lose money, you'll be in trouble.

YOU KEEP careful records of all the bets that you take. Gamblers want their money fast if they win a bet. If you keep them waiting for their money, they might turn nasty!

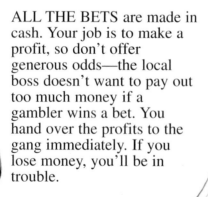

Handy Hint

Buy the latest newspaper. It prints racing results and is updated several times each day.

EACH GANG has its own "territory," or area of the city that's under its control. Always stick to your own gang's territory—if you walk around the wrong corner, you'll find yourself in serious trouble with another gang.

YOU GIVE GAMBLERS receipts for their bets. The receipts list the race they bet on, which horse they picked, how much money they bet, and how much money they will get if their horse wins the race.

11

The Gambling Den

Richer gamblers play cards, roulette, and dice games at private gambling dens. These clubs are open only to people who have been approved by gangsters. You've proved yourself to the gang, so they give you a job at a gambling den. You must dress sharply and be polite to the gamblers. You'll learn lots of new ways to part people from their money.

The gangsters arrange the games so that gamblers don't win very often. The gambling den's profits are passed on to the gang. People known to be gangsters don't work at the den—if they did, gamblers would be less likely to spend money.

I've never seen so much money!

If people only knew ...

SLOT MACHINES are designed to pay out a certain percentage of the money they take. Your job is to rig the machines so that they pay out less money.

THE ROULETTE WHEEL needs a quick-witted person to keep an eye on the wheel and on the gambling table. An experienced gang member teaches you how to run it.

POKER calls for skillful card control. You deal the cards, making sure nobody cheats by slipping a spare card out of their sleeve.

Handy Hint

Don't ever gamble. All the games are rigged so that the gang wins as much money as possible.

Better luck next time.

YOU WORK as a cashier after learning all the other jobs. The gang trusts very few people to handle so much money.

AT THE END of the day, you carry the den's profits to the gang headquarters. Watch out for rival gangsters who might try to mug you for the cash.

YOU GIVE regular reports to Tony. Your records tell him how much money is being gambled and who is doing the gambling.

Spying in the Speakeasy

Odd Jobs

ONLY PEOPLE trusted by the gang are let into the speakeasy. When you work as the doorkeeper, you have a list of these people. Don't let the wrong person in!

AS THE HOST, you introduce the glamorous singers and stage acts. You might even get to meet a Hollywood movie star!

ANYONE WHO doesn't pay for their drinks or causes trouble is thrown out. Luckily, you have tough gangsters to do this work.

THE DRINKS served in the speakeasy are wildly overpriced. The speakeasy buys only the cheapest, lowest-quality brands of alcohol. You're instructed to soak the labels off the bottles and replace them with fake labels for expensive, high-quality brands.

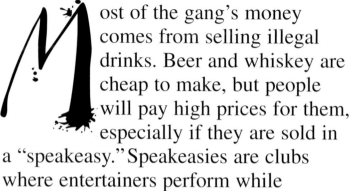

Most of the gang's money comes from selling illegal drinks. Beer and whiskey are cheap to make, but people will pay high prices for them, especially if they are sold in a "speakeasy." Speakeasies are clubs where entertainers perform while people relax, chat, and drink.

Tony tells you that the police are planning a raid on your gang's speakeasy. You let him know when the most customers and gangsters will be there, so that the police can arrest as many people as possible. But be careful not to blow your cover!

FIGHTS MIGHT break out late at night. Keep an eye out for trouble, and dive for cover if a fight breaks out.

15

Due North

Alcoholic drinks are legal in Canada, so some gangsters buy booze there and smuggle it back to the United States. Because Canadian alcohol is made legally, it is usually higher quality than the stuff made in the U.S. That means it can be sold for higher prices. You are sent north to buy a load of beer and whiskey to bring back to Chicago.

THE U.S. grants a few people import licenses, which allow them to import alcoholic beverages for medical or scientific purposes. The gangsters steal one of these licenses and make you write your own name on it.

ALL THE CASES of alcohol need to be counted and checked. You don't want any to be stolen.

IN CANADA you can relax and enjoy yourself. The gangsters can't watch what you are up to, and you are not wanted by the police. Find a nice hotel and order yourself a great meal. Wonderful stuff!

POST OFFICE LETTER BOX

YOU CAN USE the postal service without worrying that you are being watched. So you write out a complete account of everything that you have been doing recently and mail it to Tony.

The Royal Canadian Mounted Police (Mounties) can't stop you from taking drinks out of Canada—it's legal to export alcohol. But some Mounties will alert the U.S. authorities if they suspect that you're breaking U.S. law. So watch out!

Handy Hint
Study your map. If you take the wrong road, you could end up lost in the wilderness.

I think you'll find that my papers are in order, sir.

17

The Wheelman

Every gang needs a team of skilled drivers. These "wheelmen" need to know how to keep cars in top condition, how to steal cars—and above all, how to make a speedy getaway. You're being promoted quickly, and your gang is now using you as a wheelman. This means you can gather evidence as you meet important gang members and drive them around. And you will witness the gang's bank robberies, shoot-outs, and other crimes.

THE BOSS does not want you listening to his conversations. He tells you to stay out of earshot, but try to overhear as much as you can. Then you can pass the information on to Tony.

My arm is getting tired.

STAY ON your toes. The boss might keep you waiting for hours and then expect you to spring into action.

THE BOSS likes his car to be clean and shiny all the time. You will spend hours washing and waxing it.

STOLEN CARS are used during crimes. If you're ordered to steal a car, watch out for its owner!

MODERN CARS need lots of regular maintenance. You need to know basic mechanics, or you could cause more problems than you solve.

Handy Hint
Make sure you have enough gasoline—you'll need it for your getaway.

I bet Tony doesn't have to put up with this!

BATTLES WITH rival gangs are terrifying. As the wheelman, you have to get your fellow gangsters out of trouble—fast. When the bullets start flying, remember to duck!

Running the Protection Racket

Sinister Scare Tactics

SMASHING shop windows is a frequent way of punishing shop owners who do not pay on time.

IF OWNERS refuse to pay, the gang takes revenge by setting fire to their businesses, houses, or cars.

MOST owners feel they have no choice but to pay the protection money. You are sent to collect it.

IF YOU WALK into the wrong territory, rival gangsters will try to take the money you have collected. They won't ask nicely.

Soon you are asked to help run a protection racket. This is a very profitable—and very cruel and violent—way of making money. You and a pair of tough gangsters are ordered to pay a visit to a business owner. You tell him that your gang will "protect" his business against vandals and robbers—for a price. If the owner refuses to pay, you have to threaten to beat him up and vandalize his business.

Each gang runs a protection racket in its own territory, but gangs try to "muscle-in" on other gangs' turf. This can lead to battles between rival gangs. Try to stay out of these wars—they are extremely dangerous.

YOU FIND OUT which businesses the "thugs" (tough gangsters) are going to attack. Tony has been promoted to detective, so you call him to tip him off. That way he can arrest the gangsters without you being involved.

Packing Heat

It's not long before you get to meet the Big Boss. He's big, tough, and guarded by men who are "packing heat," or carrying guns. These men are hardened criminals who have been in the gang for years—they are trusted by the Big Boss. They protect him from rival gangsters and are willing to use their guns at any moment. Be careful—you don't want to get on their bad side.

CARRYING GUNS in public would attract attention from the police. Most gangsters make sure their guns are well hidden. A violin case is a useful place to hide a tommy gun.

THE BIG BOSS is head of the entire gang. All the gangsters treat him with great respect.

BODYGUARDS are mean, rude, and care only about the Big Boss. They push other people out of the way and won't listen to any complaints.

IF THERE IS a muddy puddle, the Big Boss will make you put your coat over it so that his expensive shoes stay clean.

Handy Hint

Stay out of the way of the men packing heat. They are not likely to be nice to you.

AMMUNITION is bulky and heavy, but it must be kept where the gunmen can reach it quickly. You'll find it in the most unexpected places!

YOU ARE SEARCHED by the gunmen now and then. They are looking for evidence that you are working for the police or for a rival gang.

Eh, Boss, I think I see the cops comin'.

He's clean.

He's lucky, is what he is.

Money Laundering

Money that has been stolen in bank robberies can be identified by the police by the code numbers printed on the bills. The gangsters need to exchange this "dirty" money for "clean" money in a process known as money laundering.

The bookman records the gang's money laundering in financial ledgers called "the books." The bookman has to be an accurate record-keeper and a clever mathematician. You can't believe your luck when the gangsters make you a bookman—you will learn all of the gang's secrets. That means more evidence for Tony!

THE GANG'S PROFITS are recorded in the books. That way, the Boss can make sure no one is stealing his money. Rival gangs want to get their hands on this information, so keep the books safe.

Here's your "change," sir.

GANGS RUN legal businesses in order to launder money. It's your job to deliver dirty money to your gang's store, so that it can be given out to customers as change. Some gangsters also use dirty money to buy secondhand cars, which they drive around the corner and resell for clean money.

GANGSTERS ARE PAID in clean money, to distance them from the crimes they commit. Make sure that you don't muddle up dirty money and clean money.

THE BIG BOSS will keep a close eye on the piles of cash that you handle. He'll also expect you to keep the books up to date.

You better be looking after my dough.

Handy Hint

Everyone wants the money. Don't let anyone near it. If any of it's missing, the Boss will blame you.

YOU KEEP TWO identical sets of books. One set is for the Big Boss; the other is for Tony.

The Boss

You've impressed the Big Boss so much that he's going to make you the boss of a smaller gang. Many smaller bosses have their own territories to run on behalf of the Big Boss. You will organize all the gang's activities in your territory. You now have your own bodyguards, thugs, and a bookman. You may have to do some terrible things—stealing money from anyone you can, cheating at gambling, and terrorizing business owners. You will need to watch your territory closely to stop rival gangs from muscling in to get "a piece of the action." But don't get carried away—you're still working undercover for the police!

Perks of the Job

AS A GANG BOSS, you can live in luxury—until your crimes catch up with you. Buy the very best food at the most expensive restaurants. Buy a fantastic house.

HIRE SERVANTS to look after you. Make it seem like you've earned the right to live in absolute comfort. (But remember that your money was stolen from honest folks.)

A SUDDEN BANG might be a door slamming shut, or it might be a gangster shooting at you. Living in fear is no fun, but that's life as a gangster.

Handy Hint

Search all your visitors. They might be working for a rival gang.

Listen up, knuckleheads. I run this joint now.

RIVAL GANGS will try to have you murdered, or "hit." They could try to sneak up on you at any moment.

YOU MEET with other gang bosses to discuss criminal business and make deals. Don't get cheated, or the Big Boss will be very angry.

YOU ARE expected to wear expensive clothes. Go to a tailor, and ask him to make you the very best suit he can, using only the finest cloth.

27

Final Reckoning

YOUR EVIDENCE will be crucial. Use your records to explain how the gang made money by gambling, selling alcohol, and threatening innocent people.

As soon as you have gathered enough evidence to convict the gangsters, you call in your brother, Tony. He has almost the entire Chicago police force ready for a raid. You have taken huge risks to get information on the gangsters. Now it's payback time. You arrange for the police to arrive when the Big Boss and as many gangsters as possible are present, so that they can all be arrested.

Once the trial begins, you testify about the crimes that you have seen, how they were planned, and which gangsters committed them. At last your double life as an undercover policeman is over. You have survived!

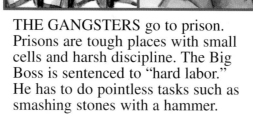

BY BUSTING THE GANGSTERS, you have made the territory they controlled safe for honest citizens. Business owners no longer pay protection money, and gunfire doesn't erupt in the street.

THE GANGSTERS go to prison. Prisons are tough places with small cells and harsh discipline. The Big Boss is sentenced to "hard labor." He has to do pointless tasks such as smashing stones with a hammer.

AFTER THE TRIAL, everyone knows you were working for the police, so your undercover career is over. You join Tony as a detective and enjoy life.

Glossary

Betting odds A number to show what a gambler could win on a bet. If the betting odds are five-to-one, the gambler could win $5 for a $1 bet.

Bootlegger A person who smuggles illegal drinks. The word comes from the fact that some smugglers hid bottles of alcohol in their boots.

Cashier A person who handles cash. In a gambling club, cashiers give customers small plastic tokens called "chips" in exchange for the money they want to bet.

Dirty money A slang term for stolen money.

Export To transport goods out of one place (usually a country) and into another.

Gangster A member of a criminal gang. Sometimes newspapers called any criminal a "gangster," even if he or she wasn't part of a gang.

Heat A slang term for a gun.

Import license A government document that gives a person legal permission to import goods from one country to another.

Jazz A style of music. It originated in the city of New Orleans, but during the 1920s it became popular across the United States.

Ledger A book in which financial records are kept.

Mountie A member of the Royal Canadian Mounted Police, which investigates serious crimes in Canada. The first Mounties rode horses, but these days, most ride in cars.

Organized crime Crime that is carried out by large groups of criminals for the purpose of making money.

Poker A card game played by gamblers.

Prohibition The banning of alcoholic drinks such as beer, wine, and whiskey. In the U.S., alcoholic drinks were banned from 1920 until 1933.

Protection racket An illegal scheme that gangsters used to make money. Gangs would make business owners pay for "protection" against thugs and thieves. If the business owner refused to pay, the gang would damage the shop or hurt the owner.

Racket A slang term for an illegal scheme to make money.

Roulette A gambling game. A ball is flicked onto a spinning wheel marked with numbers. Players bet on which number the ball will land on.

Speakeasy A private club that sold illegal alcoholic drinks. The name comes from the fact that customers would be asked to speak "easy" (quietly) when ordering a drink, in case there were undercover police in the club.

Territory The area in which a gang operates. Gangs often try to extend their territory at the expense of other gangs.

Thug A slang term for a large, violent criminal.

Tommy gun A slang term for the machine gun made by the Thompson firearms company.

Undercover police Police who disguise themselves in order to gain access to criminal organizations.

Vandalize To damage something on purpose.

Index

A
alcohol 5, 14, 16, 17
ammunition 23

B
bear 17
beer 14, 16
Big Boss 22–23, 24, 25, 26, 27,
    28, 29
bodyguards 23
bookman 24, 25
books 24, 25
bootleggers 17
bullets 19

C
Canada 16, 17
cars 18, 19
Chicago 5, 6, 7, 16
clean money 24
clothes 23, 27

D
dirty money 24
disguise 21
drivers 18, 19

E
evidence 8, 18, 24, 28, 29

F
factories 6
farms 6

G
gambling 10–11, 12–13, 26
gambling den 12–13
gang territory 11, 20, 26
gang warfare 20
guns 22, 23, 26

H
Hollywood 6, 14

I
import license 16

J
jazz music 7

L
local boss 8, 10, 18, 26

M
money laundering 24–25
Mounties 17

N
newspapers 11
numbers racket 10–11

P
poker 12
police 8, 9, 14, 26, 28, 29
prison 28, 29
Prohibition 5
protection racket 20–21, 28

R
robberies 18
roulette 12, 13
Royal Canadian Mounted Police
    17

S
slot machines 12
speakeasy 14–15

T
thugs 20, 26
tommy gun 22
trial 28

V
violin case 22

W
wheelman 18–19
whiskey 14, 16